'Til the Well Runs Dry

'Til the Well Runs Dry

Poems by
Joseph Leary

Illustrations by
Jack Leary

© 2024 Joseph Leary and Jack Leary. All rights reserved.
This material may not be reproduced in any form, published,
reprinted, recorded, performed, broadcast,
rewritten or redistributed without
the explicit permission of Joseph Leary and Jack Leary.
All such actions are strictly prohibited by law.

Cover design by Shay Culligan
Cover image by Jack Leary
Author and illustrator photos by Jack Leary

ISBN: 978-1-63980-509-9

Kelsay Books
502 South 1040 East, A-119
American Fork, Utah 84003
Kelsaybooks.com

*To my family, Susan, Kris, Jen, Dan, and Dave,
with love for so enriching my life,
and allowing me to be part of theirs.*

Acknowledgments

I wish to acknowledge the critical part played by my wife, Susan Molloy Leary, for her willingness and inexhaustible patience as the Alfa reader of these works. Her careful attention to detail was central to getting me to the finish.

I am also indebted to Kristin Leary Silber for the initial editing of this collection, to poet Matthew Lippman for his valuable guidance and encouragement, and to my friend, author, and literary agent, Donna Eastman, for providing the initial encouragement and expertise in the early going of this publication.

Finally, my gratitude to the many Beta readers who gave so generously of their time and feedback: Geraldine Lyons, Audrey Philbrick, Kristin Leary Silber, Jennifer Leary Lynch, Dan and Dave Leary, Patricia Shaw, Kristina Bray, Nancy Rappa, and Carl Ristaino.

Contents

You Don't Miss the Water 'Til the Well Runs Dry	11
Turn Out the Lights	17
The Black Onyx Ring	21
On a Snowy Morning in Middle March	26
The Guitar	29
Stop Watching Birds, Drinking Coffee, and Scrape That Loathsome Deck	32
Letting Go	35
Sometimes in My World	36
Hands	41
A Thick Black Braid	43
Ahh the Ocean	46
Takotsubo Fisherman's Trap	49
Drifting While Driving	54
The Boy in the Red Sneakers	58
Hume's Big Toe	65
Joey	75
My Window	82
Nailed It	85
Will You Still	90
Life Breaks Out	92
The Blue Birds Return	95
A Visitor Came Yesterday	98
Birdland	101
Banjo-Eyed Buzzer	106
The Talent Show	108
The Drive By	115
We Were Kids Together	119
Big Blow Storms into Town	124
Homeless Veterans	127
The Primo Protector	132
Blouse of Serious Black	134
The Mother	137
I Love	146

You Don't Miss the Water 'Til the Well Runs Dry

for Eddie

Ed was 43
Lou Gehrig's disease
snuck up and robbed him
of all but his mind
breath and laughter
a rarity in his survival
many years later he
soldiered on

Ed
Ron John and I
were young Marines together
serving in the Pacific
we often flew to visit Ed
at his home on the coast
of California just south
of Los Angeles
where he lives and laughs
with his angel wife
Charlotte who stood by
Ed when he had nothing
but his next uncertain breath

our visit finished
I set out to visit other
friends many miles away

mired in masses of
anonymous metal
exhaling their poisonous breath
I escaped the freeway
and drove north on US 395

in the low desert
of the Mohave
roadside iron towers
like giant erector sets
yoked by sagging power lines
seemed to march
along with me
striding with steely resolve
through the dull
dry expanse

passing a truck stop oasis
I stopped for a break
on offer was food . . .
and salvation
Stop Here! Classic Twinkies,
mega-sized Pepsi—and
remember—Jesus Saves!

approaching the high desert
I'd grown weary
and stopped for the night
in the Valley of Owen

on one side of the road
the snow-covered Sierras
glowed white and looked east
on the other side
the Panamint range faced
west staring back

at the Diamond Inn
in a little side office
I asked if they had a room

a tall lean man
in a ball cap sported
an Uncle Sam goatee
on his chin
making his long face
look longer

he said
*I gotta room with
a king-sized bed
last one
you can have it
for ten bucks
off my regular rate*

on the wall behind him
in a small black frame
a message for seekers
Stop a moment listen

where you headed
he asked stroking
the Uncle Sam beard
a little place up north
I said *Shingle Springs
you know it*
oh yes he said
*I lived six years in
Sacramento
passed through there often
on trips back here*

*growing up couldn't wait
to leave this place
travelled all over the world
. . . wherever I went
this place never left me*

*it's early
and still light out
too nice to stay in the room
you might could
take a short drive
fourteen fifteen miles
up into the mountains
it's quiet and there's
a coupla alpine lakes
surrounded by snow caps*

I was off turned left
then right miles down
the road not a car in sight
across the valley
then the climb up into
the mountains now
a looming presence

the road snaked
ever deeper into the heart
of the Panamints
snowy monoliths muscled up
close to the road signs
posted warnings *Avalanches
Pass at Your Own Risk*

a bend in the road
and rising before me
glowing in icy white
snow-capped mountains
formed a theater in the round
at its base twin lakes
filled alpine basins

sometimes
the world of things
feels empty parched
and brittle as if the Spring
of Life's run dry
my Spirit had grown
thirsty in need
of refreshment

I sat a silent hour
in the presence
of sparkling splendor
and slaked
my Spirit's thirst
from the deep waters
of my Well

refreshed ready
I headed back
down to the valley

stopping a moment
to listen
by a stream banked
with high desert grasses
and fed from
the alpine lakes above

the stream sang
a tumbling song
cold clear water
shifted and shimmied
flowing flowing
over around
and between the rocks
smoothing and leaving them
resting in its wake

Turn Out the Lights

for Dad

turn out the lights
if you're not using them
Dad would say
but the lights burned on

nine of us lived
in our small house
a toilet sink and tub
were cramped
and uncomplaining
in our tiny bathroom
it opened onto the kitchen

Dad worked
at the Boston Navy Yard
Mum often said
she only had eighty dollars
a week for the house
that seemed like a lot to me

once at the store
Mum asked me to help
carry these groceries
out to the car Joey
I did and returned for more
when we got back to the car
Mum was still for a moment
. . . then asked
where are the other bags

I'd put our groceries
into someone else's car
they were never returned

Dad painted the house
when he had money
for a gallon of paint
. . . it took him all summer

sometimes I sat with Dad
in the backyard
we drank Pepsi
he smoked a cigarette
it was a windy day
he took a last drag
and flipped the butt aside
it was still lit

the grass was as dry
as a desert bone that day
what a roaring blaze it was
Dad raced
through choking
sweet smoke searching
for a hose

Mum called the firemen
she stood in the yard
hands on her hips
in the distance sirens wailed
Dad said *she's royally pissed*

in 1952
Dad bought a new car
a green 1942
Hudson Super Six
it looked like a car
you'd see in the movies
speeding through
the streets of New York
a tommy gun spewing
from the passenger's window

one day Mum and I
drove passed
a group of my friends
I was embarrassed

being seen in that old car
I crouched down in my seat
Mum gave me
a sideward glance
and asked why I did that
I never did it again

sometimes
Dad grew very quiet
wouldn't speak for weeks
we all felt the silence
the lights burned on . . .
my Dad was a very good man

I wish I had known him

The Black Onyx Ring

opening
the top bureau drawer
was like looking into
the town dump

among the flotsum
and jetsum
was a deck
of forty one cards
cancelled passports
a hunting knife
in a camouflage sheath
assorted note books
a pair of dark glasses
missing a lens
and way in back
under a single brown
leather glove was a man's
black onyx ring

I remember letting go
of his hand
and seeing the ring on
the finger
of my father's right hand
as he was swallowed up
in the herd of humanity
ahead of us

the crowd was heading
for a boxing match
at a field near
our home in Dorchester

the boxing ring was nearby
glowing under flood lights
when we were separated
in dusty darkness
masses of large
shadowy men moved
this way and that
trampled the grass
and dry ground around me
clouds of dirt and dust
ballooned
seeping into my mouth
and stinging eyes

I was lost and small

I can't remember what
happened next
but the fragment of memory
is vivid and was strangely
attached to the image
of my Dad's
black onyx ring

Dad was a gentle
quiet man
wearing a wistful
look of resignation

he came home
on the 5:17 evening
train from his job at
the Boston Navy Yard

where he worked to repair
cryptographic machines
looking back
that seems a good job
for a secretive man
who kept so close to himself

every evening my
Mum would fire up our
green 1942
Hudson Super Six
and drive
to the train station
to pick him up
usually one of my six sisters
and I would tag along in
the back seat

as my Dad walked toward
our waiting car
my Mum would often say
look at your father,
he looks like a Boston Banker

and indeed he often did
wearing a gray Scala Homburg
a small gray feather
tucked in its black band
a silk neck tie with a small
tight knot at the neck
of his starched white shirt

over his dark pin-striped
suit he wore a heavy
black great coat
his shoes were shiny
black Florsheim's
and there was always
a folded newspaper
under his arm

I always thought
he looked more like
a G-man with
a tommy gun under that
great coat

Mum said he ran up
a big bill at Bond's
Clothing store to *get
that rig.*

he must have been
a man of mystery
among the small
society of regular riders
on the train ride to Boston

On a Snowy Morning
in Middle March

on this middle March morning
the stand of pines and oaks
behind our home
glistens with snow

in the light of the rising Sun
the white eastern pines
droop with the weight
of the night's snowy fall

looking from my window
in the foreground
branches of a brawny black
leafless birch
are unbent and bundled
in frosty coats of white

in the background
deep in the stand of trees
dark wings dart
from branch to branch
perching feet kick
and knock powdered snow
sending it billowing
to the understory below

the reflecting rays
of the rising Sun
are raising the heat
in the tree stand

in its core
the snow is morphing
like shape shifting Arachne
transforming snowy flakes
of crystalline dendrites and plates
into droplets of falling water
to begin the long journey
back to the bosom
of mother Thalassa

later now
the trees
have shed their ermine coat
and birds are attacking
the feeders
and looking forward to spring
soon a rafter
of hen and tom turkeys
will parade onto the scene
in their gobbling
turkey trot way

at the feeder
a wintering robin eats
dried mealy worms
and wonders where
warm wrigglers
might be writhing

The Guitar

for Dan

the guitar sits mute
strings taut
patiently waiting
a lover's searching fingers
to bring to life its music
yet there it sits on its pod
a melancholy image

my son
now grown
brought it to me
he said
maybe we could share
the music Dad
fathers and sons
how we strive
to touch each other

I remember now
my confusion—
how I thought I could
make a boy a man
his early teens
the quiet rage
of his resistance
the dissonance
of my insistence

back then in his bedroom
fist holes in the plaster
underlying slats
exposed like a
wounded creature's ribs
he fought to find his voice
in his new Gibson guitar

I was so young myself
tone deaf
I could hardly
sing my own song . . .
how could I hear his

in time his music came
and not too soon
he struggled to stay afloat
dragged down
by the expectations
of others

with his Gibson
like a weather bell tolling
guiding in the maelstrom
of stormy thoughts and
the tossing waves
of young emotions
he made his way

and I made mine
changed and weathered now
I've heard life's outer
and inner music
and I feel
a certain harmony

if I learn the language
of the strings
and if we listen closely
may be in time
we'll hear each other's song

Stop Watching Birds, Drinking Coffee, and Scrape That Loathsome Deck

the scabrous deck
is a clear rebuke
to proper form and order
oblivious
its owner sits
swilling cups of coffee

and watching birds
flitting round their feeders

nearby his wife casting
sidelong glances at the deck
remarks *what a sorry mess*
looks like a loathsome
skin disorder
and to emphasize
her diagnosis she slams
the sliding screen door shut

the owner
sits silent minutes
carefully composing
a proper manly answer
to such a provocation

after due deliberation
he says in whining tones
can't a man enjoy
his coffee without
listening to that crapola

in his mind
a dismal image is slowly
taking shape a deck
of football field dimensions
appears with layers
of peeling curling paint
its surface looks cadaverous
and in the end zone he sits
a scraper in his hand

she's right he thinks
so what's to do
with firm resolve he gathers

scrapers long and short
whisk brooms
pans and buckets
and puts an edge back
on his putty knife

he stands forlorn
before the squalid scene
reluctant to get started
the task seems overwhelming
he needs a bit of motivation
—a flash of grace
and to himself he says
I agree with wise Lao Tzu
a journey starts
with just single step

with that he consecrates
the lowly job before him
on hands and knees
he senses satisfaction
as he works
his sharp-edged putty knife
and with a single stroke
he slides it forth
then back then side to side
he pauses pleased to see
a strip of paint
give way before him

Letting Go

there
in the market parking lot
on the cusp of winter's bite
stands a tree
smallish and young
still clutching
curled and lifeless leaves
refusing to give way to
winter's death-like sleep
I understand
it's frightening to let go
to surrender control . . .
you never had

Sometimes in My World

in my world an old man sits
watches his son dance
with his daughter of five
they sing laugh and strum
their air guitars
the old man sees himself
and smiles

in my world I listen
while an old man
weaves his tale
for bar mates
and sips whiskey
at Poor Red's bar in El Dorado

once upon a time he began
I was a welterweight
on a Marine Corps
boxing team
he punctuates this
with a lightening
flurry of two-handed
air jabs
my dad taught me
to fight
another flurry of jabs

and a quick breath
he was small my dad
but tough and cocky
a regular bantam rooster

he was a fisherman too
we had an old boat
caught lots of fish
ate all we could

he made me clean the rest
I hated cleaning the fish
I hated him

times were tough
we carried the leftover fish
to hungry widowed women
a great guy my dad
a flurry of air jabs

in my world
on a dreamy drive
along the saw-toothed
mountains
of the Sierra Nevada
I stopped
for a wind-burned
old man
sitting by the roadside
he was wearing
a t-shirt shorts
and knee-high boots

to an offer of help
he said *yes*
would you please
go to the laundromat
near the fire station
up the road
tell Sandy

in the brown Tundra
that Mort came out
down the road

that's all I asked
yes that's it he said
squinting in the glare
of the snowy slopes

after hiking
in snow covered foothills
Mort was in need of a ride
I passed no one
on my drive up the road

at the laundromat
no Sandy
at the fire station
no Tundra
returning to tell Mort
there was no Sandy
no Tundra,
there was no Mort
was he just
a mountain ghost
on my misty
mountain drive

in my world
I pause in my day
to notice
oak trees swaying
greeting the coming Spring

I feel the still chilled air
see buds swelling
at the tips
of bare gray limbs

in the high branches
silhouetted against
floating white patches
in a pale blue sky
a squirrel hops and stops
hops and stops

in my world
my friend Jim a vet
eight years in a wheelchair
walked
seventy-two steps today
three months ago
he couldn't walk one
in my world that's
cause to celebrate

Hands

hands
what a miracle
of movement and power
these strange terminal units
with their pentadic projections
at the end of your arm

hands
with fingers closed in a fist
to pummel punish and smash

hands
that fire a backhanded blow
trailing the whiff of whiskey breath

or hands
with their finely tuned fingers
sensing two coffee filters
when only one is needed

or hands
with fingertips tracing
the course of a lip or a breast

or hands
touching the face
and tousling the hair

or hands
extended with upward facing palms
fingers spread in an offer of openness

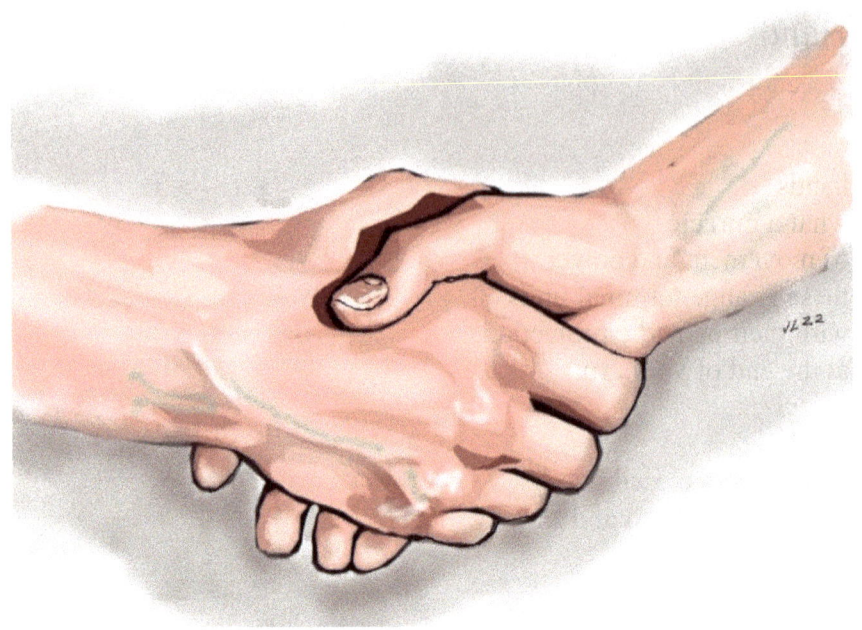

or hands
reaching out to join with another

or hands facing each other
in a silent triangle of supplication

A Thick Black Braid

it's April
early morning
in the market parking lot

pull throughs
often scarce as hen's teeth
abound just now
shoppers stride
toward the market
in cool fresh air

the sort of freshness
that engulfs you
when you suck in the scent
of wafting clothes
drying on a line
in the sun

in the market
the shoppers breeze
along the empty aisles
eyeballing products
as endless as buffalo
on the plains

bumblebee busy
pushing my cart
I notice a sturdy woman
in a rose-colored blouse
logoed in crossed baguettes
and wearing a watch cap
striped in red
a single braid of
thick black hair falling
in the back to her waist

with care she piles
pears and peaches
apples oranges and grapes
on a stand
while the Earth whirls
on its axis
racing round the Sun
sixty-seven thousand miles
in an hour

the Sun
his sisters
Venus and Uranus
his brothers
Mars Jupiter and the rest
are no more than specks
in the flailing outer arm
of a small spiral galaxy
spinning
a hundred miles
in a second 'round its
own black hole

joining billions
of other galaxies
dervishes dancing
in the darkness
of the universe

sometimes
in such moments

I find it hard to locate
my self-importance

Ahh the Ocean

it's a fine thing indeed
strolling along the beach
where the heaving Atlantic
wets the sleeve
of the continent
my feet heel deep
in soft soggy sands
marking a passage
soon washed away
in the waves
like my life
in the tides of time

it's especially grand
when the surf is high
and singing
a full-throated
song of the sea
and gulls joining the fun
screeching swooping
and diving
and the wind
the misty wind
wafting salty fragrances
of mother Thalassa
while skittering sandpipers
race surging retreating wavelets

strewn about
are remains
of the ocean dead
decaying denizens
horseshoe crabs flipped
on their backs
like beetles
their soft underbellies
exposed
and gull-gutted
cast off empty shells once
the home of fat juicy clams

eyeless fish
sockets staring
now food for the living

ahh to be alive
wind on my face and hair
sucking in scents of salty air
deep blue waves
sun sparked and twinkling
like sea-born jewels
their leading lips curling
and breaking white

Takotsubo Fisherman's Trap

for Mary Alice

octopus
a creature skilled
in camouflage
shape shifting
and inky getaways
Neptune's
undulating genius
all whooshs and waves

and yet

she's seduced
by the simplicity
of the takotsubo
a fisherman's trap

a narrow-necked jar
entices
the bubble-headed
predator with
the prospect of
luscious privacy
comfort and darkness

slipping into
the sea-bottom pottery
she drapes
her boneless body
into the thick
pitch black solitude
and

dreams
of dancing
on the sea floor
bouncing
on her eight legacles
flashing angry reds
to enemies and
shy sky blues
and rich earthy
orange browns
to friends
and plays in
tentacle tangles
with her beloved

until

jarred awake
by a tug
another and
an another still
she's dragged
in her cozy jar
up up up
breaking the boundary
between water and air
to enter a world
of breathless horror

she'll pay
denominated in pain
for her comforts
her transient serenity
to settle the eternal
accounts of this for that

she's not alone
in having
to settle accounts
the human heart hosts
a symphony
of pleasure pain
love and loss and

seeking solace
finds love joy
refuge and comfort
in the presence and
quiet depths
of another's heart
sharing in
the mystery
of existence . . .

yet

it comes with strings
ties from another world
where a debt of happiness
has been created
that calls for balance
to be restored
the price

heartbreak

one day comes a tug
from a world beyond
snatching the heart

of her love and refuge
her heart swells
in grief

a vascular knot
tightens
around the neck
of her swelling ventricle
leaving her breathless
weak for months

in her broken heart
her strangling ventricle
is the mirror image of
the takotsubo

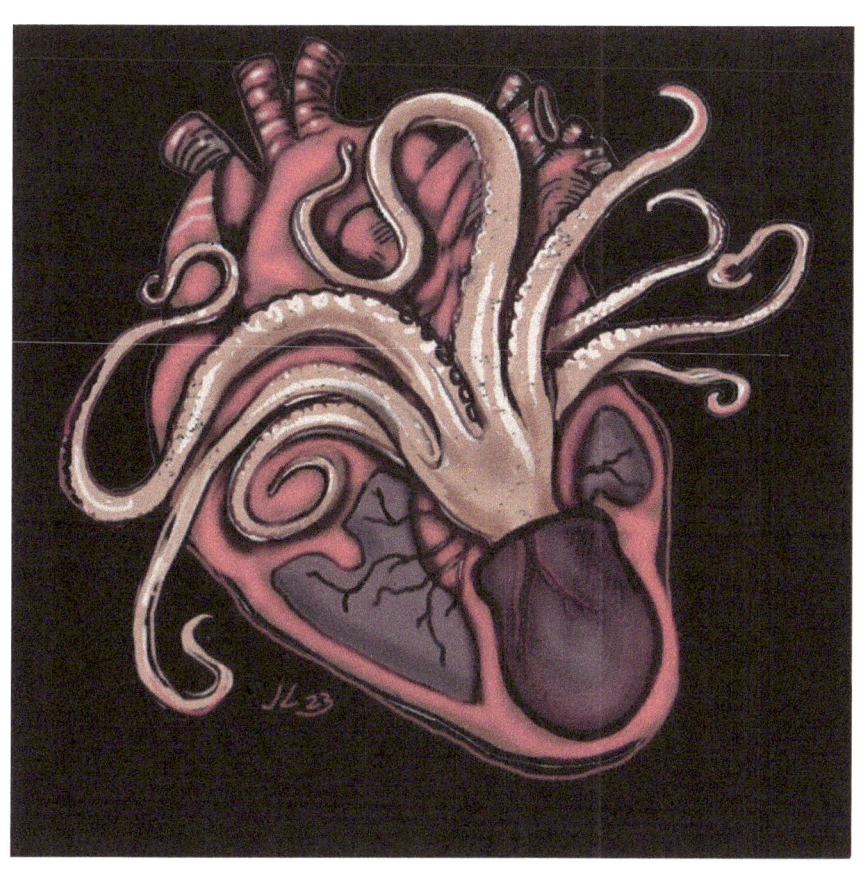

Drifting While Driving

once on a time
when my frontal lobes
had long since matured
and my brain
such as it is
was fully capable
my Mind
in its customary state
bobbled along
on a sea of thought
as I drove to work

we human creatures
have an amazing capacity
to carry on while we inhabit
inner worlds of thought
popping back and forth
between a dream-like world
and what some call
the Now

seen from this Now
we appear to be present
wide awake
driving talking walking
without collision

yet we're often on automatic
cruising floating along
in a land of near sleep

on that long ago day
the drive to work
was the usual experience
leaving home
arriving intact in the parking lot
with no clear memory
of how I got from one place
to the other

it's not uncommon
but sitting in the car
I felt for the first time
then I knew
what it is to be present
I could see in an instant
that much of life is spent
dreaming dramas
lost in the world of thought
like the shadowy figures
in Plato's cave

later I saw too
that strong emotions
like anger
create similar states
where one is swamped
in a tsunami of emotion
no longer present
and for the moment
seemingly hijacked

one even says
I was carried away
I wasn't myself
I was out of my mind
where did my *I* go
I wonder

sometimes
stepping awake
from the dream world
into the *Now*
if only for an instant
we may get to see
behind the curtain
and glimpse
the wizard of I
a bit more clearly

to be aware
in such a moment
and to wonder
what lies beyond the I
is to be touched
is to be granted a moment
of life changing grace

The Boy in the Red Sneakers

the old man
scratching his travel itch
is visiting Japan
with his daughter
and two grand
daughters

in the Tomigaya
neighborhood of Tokyo
the ghosts of Dōgen
and Confucius
drift and touch

meditative merchants
mindful in their shops
of vintage clothing
tea bars
gastro pubs and more
and welcome
the old man and his daughter
with *arigato gozaimasu*

the old man
tires with standing
and traipsing
from shop to shop
they stop for coffee at
Beasty Coffee lab

in the shop
numbers of
sleek looking professionals
handsome

with thick and shiny
black hair
are generally dressed in
darks
while quietly making
digital love
to their computers

approaching the side
of the counter
they are wordlessly
redirected
to the proper position
with a wave of the hand

on the menu
they point
and place an order

a detached young man
in a loose gray smock
nods
they count out their yen
and take their seats
at a two chair table

a fragrance of incense
with notes of
cinnamon clove
and myrrh mix
with the silence
in the spotless space

the old man
watches
as the barista
in a black smock
prepares the coffee
in a spirit of stillness
hands flowing
his movements
smooth deliberate
and unhurried
like a priest
celebrating Mass

a narrow stream
of hot water appears
from the mouth
of a gooseneck kettle
streaming in discrete
concentric circles
over the grounds
teasing out
the dark essence
of coffee within

when ready
the barista flows
cat-like between
tables to place
the cups before them
turning the
handle of each cup
to the proper pickup
position

later
they shoot off
on a bullet train
to Kyoto
the *city of shrines*
to wander through a craft fair
in sunny Umekoji Park
near Kyoto Station

the old man
weary with heat
and walking
sits to rest

on a stone wall
his body filling with
relief
like the rising
tide of pleasure
in a gentle orgasm

he is aware
of becoming

less

his gait no longer
fluid
his hearing no longer
acute
his mind no longer
quick
his stamina
seeping away

he begins
to see himself
as others see him now

an old man
exchanging the gift
of experience
for his physical gifts

a boy
in red sneakers
is chasing
a yellow butterfly

the butterfly
slips and slides
zigs and zags
upping and downing
the boy whoops
with a sense
of boundless
energy
a love of the run
and the chase

leaving the park
on a train ride far
below the city surface
next to him
sits a young girl
doing her little girl thing

she slouches wriggles
hands now
rubbing her head
now fingering her ear
now pulling her lip
now whining

her father shushes her
gently
takes her hands in his
and puts them down
in her lap
she straightens
becomes quiet

the only sound
the train
rocking slightly
whooshing along
the tunnel darkness
lids slip over eyes
cell phones threaten
to fall
from sleeping hands

Hume's Big Toe

for Kris

they wandered
along the Royal Mile
where Edinburgh Palace
is perched high upon
Castle Rock
crouched like
a stony yellow-eyed
bird of prey
threatening to pounce

the site's been occupied
by humans—
and possibly others
—since the Iron Age
long long before
old leather-arse died
fiddle in hand

gaping tourists gathered
wondering if
their sweet old Queen
was up there in that
dark and drafty
pile of rocks
shivering in the shadow
of a smoldering fireplace

the palace dates back to
king David 1 of Scotland
known to his court as
Dauíd mac Maíl Choluim
but we'll just call him Dave

a twelfth century worthy
Dave appears in a Wikipedia
illustration ringed by an
ouroboros
and ensconced
on his sturdy throne
a sword in one hand
an orb or a grapefruit
in the other
he's wearing a pair
of men's size 26
fashionable pointy slippers

he's narrow
of shoulder and shin
and looks vaguely cross-eyed
perhaps fearing that his palace
which sits atop an old volcano
plugged with a mass
of black basaltic lava—
is in fact an early version
of a Saturn rocket
poised for blast off
carrying his own dear self
—and the palace into space
to take its place in
Vincent's starry starry night

oh the very tot's enough
to cross ye'z eyes

further on
David Hume
sits upon his plinth
in weighty metallic silence
dressed
in greenish-gray patina
save for one bright bronzy
and slightly flexed big toe
inviting travelers or
perhaps a passing podophile
to touch it
in the hope of securing
a golden future
or at least
a fleeting fling with a foot

Joseph and Kristin
father and daughter
seeking to uncover
long-buried
Scottish roots
torn from the rocky soil
of Barra in the Outer Hebrides
during an 18th century
forced immigration
to make room
for grazing sheep

Figure 1 Joe wondering about the toe *are ye kiddin' me*

Figure 2 Kristin *seeking good fortune*

they wandered on
among clusters
of gray-black buildings
stained with
the smoke of centuries
and into Old Town
and Greyfriars Kirkyard
said to be home
to 100,000 dead

it's not a large place
they must be stacked
shoulder to shoulder
belly to belly
twenty feet deep

a story is told
that one John Gray
aka Auld Jock was
once the watchman
at the olde graveyard
where he shared
his lonely nights
with Bobby
a Dandie Dinmont Terrier
and his loyal friend
to the end . . . *and beyond*

sitting
in the graveyard darkness
puffing his pipe
the glow of fired tobacco
rising and falling in the bowl

Jock would notice Bobby
head cocked ears erect
peering into the darkness
and humming a low whine

in such moments
Jock swore he could hear
olde leather arse playing his
fiddle in distant shadows
over the sound
of murmuring and shuffling feet

he wondered
could it be the dead dancing
in the light of the moon
rising over the palace
high above on Castle Rock

the story goes on that when
Auld Jock finally gained
membership
in Greyfriars Kirkyard's
exclusive club of dead

Bobby—a shaggy-haired
little lad bursting with energy
tail wagging at warp speed
throwing good natured feints
left right and forward
the very essence
of cuteness incarnate
—made it his doggy business
for the next 14 years

to prowl and sniff
around the spot where
Auld Jock was pancaked
atop a stack
of the long-buried
and when a cannon
boomed at mid-day
from the heights of
Castle Rock

Bobby seemingly enchanted
by his growing legend
set out at a run
to the site where for years
he and Auld Jock
often had their lunch

oh what a 'ting it was

when people flocked
from wide and far
to see that loveable loyal
Bobby bounding from
Greyfriars Kirkyard
ears flopping in the dash
to meet long dead Jock
for a bite of goose liver

and what a racket
them people made with
their oooing and ahhhing
enough to wake the dead
by Jove

and what a treat
it must have been
to see Auld Jock—
curious and aggravated
by all the top-side doings
—cause ripples
in the grass and dirt
above his resting place

then

to see him rising
from atop his stack
of twenty deep
as a moldy Lazarus
with bits of flesh hanging
from his yellowing bones
like socks on a drying rack

oh wonderous day and
how Kristin and Joe
marveled at the story
of a dog as loyal and faithful
as a marching mailman
as they dug into
their grill cheese and fries
washing it down
with a pint of pale lager

Joey

for Joey B

sunday morning papers
scanning the obituaries
a name catches my eye
a long-buried memory
stirs rises as in a dream

a moonless winter night
a boy of ten
stands with his mother
before a set of stairs

atop the stairs a door
a drape of crepe
behind lace-curtained
windows something
colored soft red
flickers

we need to go in now
the mother whispers to the boy
I'm afraid Mum
they begin to climb
frozen stairs that crack
and echo
in the icy silence

months before this night
the boy and his family
moved from Boston to
the countryside in Franklin
the boy was excited

to move
but sad leaving
his friend Joey behind

he and Joey used to
rough-house
tumbling side to side
among linen bundles
in the laundry van
that Joey's father drove

on playground swings
they'd pump and push
reaching for the clouds
and sometimes
in summer twilight
after supper
they'd run together
chasing the chiming
ice cream truck

in the Franklin countryside
woodchucks skunks
and pheasants roamed
and wild grape vines
clambered up the trees

in a stream
nearby his home
the boy gently
poked a turtle
thinking
what fun we'll have
when Joey comes to visit

one gray day
crouched beside the stream
watching crayfish scuttle
he hears his mother calling
across the field

they sit in silence
in the house

in time
she takes his hand
saying softly
Joey's sick
he's in the hospital

on swings
in the hospital courtyard
they pump and laugh
reaching for the sky
just as they did before

nearby
the mothers sit
shaded by trees
heads down
in quiet talk

weeks pass
again they visit Joey
this time
Joey's in a bed
he smiles a little
but he's mostly quiet

where was his hair

late autumn
winter's here
trees seem to be
in mourning
dying leaves
in spirals falling
join the softness
of earth

the boy watches
birds peck
juiceless grapes
his mother's voice
echoes again
across the field

in the kitchen
they sit their stillness
till at last she says
Joey died this morning

now standing before
the crepe-draped door
he wonders
what's behind
the curtained windows
that flickers muted red

we need to go in now
his mum repeats
urging him forward
don't be afraid
it's time
time to say goodbye
to Joey
she rings the bell

inside
a hush of voices
the door slowly opens
Joey's mother standing
hands before her face
as if in prayer
she reaches out

in the darkness within
a strange box stands in
a cone of softened light
embraced by flowers
fat red candles
flicker and drip
at either end

the box is open
yawning wide
the cover lined
in ivory-colored cloth
a heavy smell
of flowers smothers

Joey's face is pale
his head resting
on a silky pillow
the boy wonders
is Joey only sleeping

he looks 'til
he can look no more
then
Joey's mother whispers
he's happy now
in heaven

where is that
he's thinking and
wasn't Joey happy here

My Window

poached eggs eaten
coffee steaming in my cup
trying to digest
the hard to swallow
morning news
a floating airfield
slices through the Yellow Sea

mankind's fate
packed in bombs
beneath the deck
the captain
in his conning tower
ponders Oppenheimer
quoting Vishnu

now I am become Death
the destroyer of worlds

nearby on the Korean peninsula
Kim with a scary smile
and scarier haircut watches
from his concrete bunker
and offers starving masses
missiles—chew on that!

but in my window
on the world
a flowering pear tree
bursting white
fills the sashes
a bride of spring
she waits
the hand of summer
while Earth pirouettes
round father Sun

father Sun
his whirling brood in tow
clings to Orion's flailing arm
spinning along the Milky Way
the Milky Way in turn
tiptoes round its own black hole
and joins the speeding galaxies
spinning in infinitude

please is there any coffee left

Nailed It

the crowd was raucous
that night at Fenway Park
the diamond glittering like day
the smell of cigars and popcorn
drifted in the air
the pitcher coiled in his windup
unleashed a fast ball

a crack split the din
echoed through the park
the guy selling hot dogs
turned to look
everyone jumped to their feet
I couldn't see a thing
Dad said *he nailed it*

high on the hard seats
of Boston Arena
I sat swinging my foot
toeing a black wad
of gum on the concrete floor

in the ring below
in a cone of light
fighters danced clinched
bobbed and punched

Dad said *it's the prelim*
the smell of sweat
drifted up with the squeak
of boxing shoes on canvas
scattered boos bubbled
in the darkness

one of the fighters
was a tall skinny guy
named Paul
someone yelled *hey Paul*
throw me up a rib
Dad said *catching Paul*
was like nailing
Jello to a tree

in a flash
a fat gloved hand shot out
Paul's head jerked back
his long legs buckled
he sank to the canvas
in eagle spread
Dad said *he nailed him*

when I was ten
we moved to Franklin
in the country
there was a dairy farm
across the road
whose fields were full
of dewy-eyed cows
and fierce looking
big-balled bulls

I learned broken field
running there
dodging frisbee shaped
dollops of dung

sometimes I helped
at a chicken farm
nearby our house
urine laded
wood shavings carpeted
the chicken coop floor

the coop door squeaked
when it opened
startled chickens squawked
sprung into the air
with wing-beaten clouds
of dust and feathers
the smell of ammonia
made my eyes water
took my breath away

deep in the woods
I often heard the raspy honk
of wild pheasant
I ached to find them

one day as I stood
in the field behind our house
a gray hen pheasant
led her brood
from the nearby wetlands

the little family stopped
a few feet from me
twittering and chucking

slowly slowly
I picked up a rock
paused—and threw it

in a chaos
of fluttering wings
all but one bird flew off
I stared a while
at the lump on the ground
walked forward
picked up the bird

its head swung
on a limp neck
the body was soft
still warm
yes . . . *I nailed it*

Will You Still

in the floor an open vent
nearby
in a closely woven carpet
adrift in its weave
faded images
of blossom walled wombs
and Vishnu seated
atop flaming mandalas
intertwined with leaves
and flowers

the vent sighs deeply
through the parted lips
of its grille
the rising warmth
enfolds
a Venetian blind above

the skin of its vinyl slats
aglow with the touch
of early morning sunshine
the vent's soft breath
stirs the slats
creating a dance
of shadows and light
embracing

rising and falling together
in rolling waves like
the tangled loins of lovers

while from the Sonos
in the background
the Shirelles wonder
Will You Still
Love Me Tomorrow

Life Breaks Out

it's spring again
a few weeks ago
the flowering pear tree
across the street
stretched its naked limbs
toward the warming sun
buds locked for months
in winter's icy grip are
swelling pushing yearning
to breakout
—to be

yesterday
I drove by Walpole Prison
concrete and heavy
in its place at Cedar Junction

twenty feet above the ground
atop thick gray walls
humming wires threaten
eight hundred bodies
living encased there
but life's spirit can breakout
knows no walls
—is free

beyond the prison
a stream flows beneath a road
it bubbles and chortles
into a marsh beyond

on its sandy bottom
crayfish meander
walking sideways
over water-polished stones

stands of cattails
with brown banger
seed heads
taking shape in clusters
beside elfin-eared
pods of milkweed

which
swell burst and spill
their silky seeds
to drift away
carrying packages of
life's potential

last night in a quiet moment
an image came to me
a lotus flower
rising from a murky pool
opens blooms
and in its brief moment
offers gifts
of color fragrance and
notions of renewal

petals dropping
it slowly fades away

The Blue Birds Return

tucked away in a room
surrounded by bookshelves
I'm alive with old friends
Heaney Dickinson Dostoyevsky
and hundreds more

they sit shoulder to shoulder
silent between their covers
waiting their turn to share
poetry stories and wisdom
while Ray Charles
and Count Basie bang out
Oh What a Beautiful Morning

this celebration of being
blossoms
in the bookish space
sunshine angles
through Venetian blinds
mixing with the warmth
of the flickering fireplace

outside
trees stretch their gray
leafless limbs sunward
offering the life
in their swelling buds
for a touch
of springtime's radiance

swooping and dipping
in flashes of lapis lazuli
the Bluebirds are back

enticed by warm winter days
the prodigals return
from the warmth
and lazy places
where insects abound
and sing deep into the
night beyond twilight

break out the mealy worms
fill feeders to overflowing
the Blue Birds have returned

but oh those mourning doves
muscling out the songbirds
bobbing their heads
and wearing gray suits
intolerable

listen to the pretentious
sadness of their song
sad only in failing to snatch
every sunflower seed in sight

and those turkeys
squirrels and starlings
so maddening
to have to abide
the good with the bad
. . . such a nuisance

A Visitor Came Yesterday

arriving in fits and starts
first rain then snow
snow and more snow

as gray light drained
the air came alive
with tumbling flakes
a crystalline curtain
twisting in the roar
slanting flakes
flew sideways
thick oaks swayed
flexing anchored roots
while naked limbs
whipped and snapped
hailing the coming storm

all night the blizzard blew
while tucked in a treetop drey
of dead leaves and branches
a squirrel snugged
and drew its furry
tail in tighter

morning opened
wrapped in white
birds darted swooping
from bush to tree
to hanging feeders

a sparrow flitted
found a perch
looked up
then right then left
plucked a fat
black sunflower seed
and flew away

his holiness
the cardinal
in red imposing
made his entry
more modest came
the juncos wrens
and black-capped
chickadees

in the east
the sun climbed slowly
painting winter skies
in hues deep blue
cloudy clusters
white and puffy
drifted in the bluing

in the treetop drey
a stirring
snow slightly shifting
slid billowing to earth
hungry squirrels chirping
scamper headlong
round and down
the tree trunk

hopping pausing
flagging tails
they dashed across
the crusty snow
and gathered seed
fallen from the feeders

startled mourning doves
scurry hop and
flap their modo wings

Birdland

it's dawn in our backyard
a time when the quiet
is so loud
you can hear it
when light and dark create
a magic mixture
the moment of change
between past and future
as Earth pirouettes and
turns us toward
the fiery face of the Sun

it snowed last night
there are tufted titmice
and shiny blackbirds
in the woods
these early morning singers
are riffing
in tweets and twitters
joining with other bird songs
to create a sun rising symphony

story has it
that once upon a time
in a Kansas City park
young Charlie Parker
often joined the early birds

in the dawning chorus
adding the sound
of his alto sax
to the cacophony
of life's gathering sound
riffing returning
riffing and returning
always tending toward balance

resolving into euphony
neighbors round the parkland
came to call him 'Bird'

while the sun graces
our yard with
his gentle early light
I prepare our breakfast
my wife makes her way
through snow
carrying her pail
of dried mealworms
shelled sunflower seeds
and hard and white
seeds of safflower
to fill feeders in our birdland

we eat our breakfast
while outback
bluebirds finches
and black-capped chickadees
swoop and charge the feeders
the scene's aflutter
with dark forms
like musical notes
escaping from a paper score
and dancing in the air

the flutter of wings
the riffing of songs
and returning rhythms
are enough
to make Bird's big heart
swell and sing

skittish birds
dart flash and hover
wing-beating one another
to clear a busy perch

bobbing heads
check the sky
peck pause
and check the sky again
and flying flit away

on a nearby tree top
a hawk sits in silence
her eyes unblinking
focused on feeders
far below like tables
set for a feast

in an instant
the hawk pushes off
her tree-top perch

in gliding silence
a long descent
wings spread
legs thrust forward
talons deployed
poised sharp and ready

suddenly
a wing-shaped shadow
falls across the feeders
like the darkness
that shadowed Bird's
brief life

chaos
engulfs the feeders
beating wings explode
feathers fly
birds flee in all directions

a black-capped
chickadee chirps
struggles briefly in the grip

of crushing talons
the hawk
its prey secure
takes one step
hops
thrusts upward airborne
on flexing pulsing wings

Banjo-Eyed Buzzer

I hear buzzing
in a cluster
of multi-colored Dahlias
a humble bumble bee
is bouncing
from blossom to blossom
doing her work
with style and esprit
stuffing her corbiculae
with corn-yellow pollen

this banjo-eyed beauty
is agile
given her look
of a pint-sized
boxcar with wings

she's content
to rise for work
as Earth is turning
to face the waiting sun
and at the end of day
to trim her wings
and antennae and
drift off in the early
evening darkness
to the comforting hum
of the hive

The Talent Show

for Caitlin

in the school auditorium
the first ten rows
are a tumble of talk
amid ear shattering
screams of support
that rocket
out of the buzz

silhouetted
in the twilit hall
busy bodies dash
here then there

on stage
intense teachers smile
finagle with mikes
and sound systems
performers dart
in and out of the wings
waving to friends
in the front rows

the countdown begins
five four three two . . .
the drone
in the ten row hive
ebbs and flows
into silence

enter right
three young emcees
perky and loud

in deliberate voices
they lay out the intro
of upcoming acts
the ten-row hive erupts
in stamping approval
the floor trembles

in their turn
musicians finger keys
and strings
drummers tap out rhythms
vocalists vibrate cords
gymnasts split tumble
and flip across the stage
dancers dance in
a harmony of movement

some kids
confident cocky
have found their home
others
are halting uneasy
hoping just to make it through
to escape evaluating eyes
peering from the darkness

parents are whiplashed
now proud
now squirming
in heartache
as misplaced mikes
give us silent lip syncs
drumsticks beating
soundless drums

alone
in the spotlight
center stage
a singer
in a flowered dress
hands by her side
fingers softly pulling
at her dress seams
awaits her music

in time the
music begins
her voice rising
shoulders slightly hunched
she says to the audience
that's not my music

her music lost
in the sound system
the hall and hive fall silent
a teacher rushes center stage
comforting rescuing
she'll be back
to sing her lovely song

the show moves on

a girl hip-spins
fiery red and gold
hula hoops
and while the hoops
are spinning
her hands and feet

add serial dances
to create a symphony
of movement

new music begins
the sweet metallic
bounce of the Ranat
fills the air

soon to be softened
by the plaintiff cry
of the two string
So Duang

in a sari golden red
Caitlin stands
a closed fan in hand
she wings it open
with a snap revealing
the fiery red of a rising sun
then rolls it closed
like the dazzling dance
of a Bird of Paradise

atop her head a crown
of golden spikes
bursting blossoms
of sunbeams
radiate from a bun
of black and silky hair

her dance begins
hands appear
as if solitary creatures

fingers pulse and
flex like the remiges
of coasting hawk wings
tipping and dipping
on a rising thermal

slowly one foot
lifts turns pauses
is placed
followed by the other
the movement
serpentine smooth
and soft

as if floating
she glides her dance
about the stage

the hive watches
quiet entranced
until she stops
cocks her head and
snaps her fiery fan shut
and the spell is broken

two young gents
mosey up
to a lemonade stand
lift their boater hats
in greeting and start
to sing the Duck Song

suddenly the hive awakens
shifting in their seats
awash in childhood memory
they join the lemonade lads

A duck walked up
to a lemonade stand
And he said to the man,
running the stand hey . . .

and soon the hall
was filled
with merry song

The Drive By

it's springtime
in Covidaville
before micronic masses
hitched a ride
and washed up
on our shores

our country road
was quiet
and rarely hosted
those who walk
or jog

it's curious how
those little buckaroos
have suddenly awaken us
we've been in a dither
these past two years
newly aware
of our fragility
our lives no more
than wavering
candle flames . . .
so easily blown out

long confined
we've grown grateful
and pine for simple joys
fresh air
a change of scene
for people walking by
for wind in the trees
as it is today

re-minding us
of rising tides
and curling waves
beating on misty shores

my window frames
a background of
ocean-blue bright skies
adrift with clustered
white topped
shadow bottomed clouds

in the foreground
a trio of teenaged oaks
is swaying waving
crowns of popcorn buds

the road below is empty
but in the distance
there's a sound
a cacophony
of morse coding horns
coming closer

a car appears
followed by
another and another
a merry din is rolling by
bouncing balloons
trail from
open windowed cars
smiling kids shout
wave handmade

paper signs all
wishing happy birthday
to the lad who
lives next door

it's a drive-by

the birthday boy
all nine years of him
stands on the lawn
Mum behind him smiling
hands on his shoulders

in time this rolling party
will pop from his tangle
of memories marking
the days of the plague

the caravan
continued snaking
round the cul-de-sac
a bright spot
in the darkness

in days of darkness
my long dead
Irish mother
would have said
Joey dear it's true
'tis an ill wind
that blows no good

We Were Kids Together

I remember the day
you were delivered
we were kids together
I was ten
you were cute with
your small round screen
and rabbit like ears

your flickering
black and white pictures
and big cloth-covered
speakers
out there for all to see

and your shows
how you delighted
and made us laugh
the tv god who created you
rightly named you Zenith
for me you were the tops

I turned you on
and you turned me on
to *Time for Beany*
and his buddy Cecil
the seasick sea serpent

and Buster Crabbe
as Flash Gordon
blasting off
in his space ship
supported by visible wires

and that hokey puppet
Howdy Doody
sitting on Buffalo Bob's lap
and who could forget
the ever creepy
Clarabell the Clown
honking and spraying
seltzer at Bob
how innocent
how easily entertained
we were back then

it was even more fun
to watch you explore
your boundaries
producing more
mature programming

your shows had color now
were more self-conscious
but we still had *Milton Berle*
I Love Lucy and Jackie Gleason
doing vaudeville and
serving up slapstick

and setting us straight
was Joe Friday
who gently introduced us
to your seamy underside
with his
just the facts ma'am routine

while *Walter Cronkite* shared
deep-space knowledge
so humanity could blast off
with the astronauts
when man left earth
and gave us comfort
grounded us when *JFK*
was felled

and he helped us
cope with reality
reassuring us saying
and that's the way it is
. . . life was truly grand
and so were you

now you've come of age
mature confident
in your sophistication
your giant screen
dominant demanding sleek
stylish and smart

now you call
your shows *content*
and producers *capture*
viewers saying
whatever gets eyes gets time

sometimes
you can be crass and loud
bringing us Jerry Springer
sometimes
you're boring repetitious
giving us fluff
like the Bachelor
sometimes
you are calm and lovely
taking us into Nature
sometimes
you're all of this
like me a regular adult
. . . welcome to the family

Big Blow Storms into Town

the storm corkscrews
up the coast
Cassandra warnings
charge the air
weather prophets hover
stirring entrails
casting bones
blowing smoke

asking
what will be the weather
and whether we can
weather this raging storm
will blizzards blizz
will gales wail

winds are winding
screwing 'round and 'round
snowflakes flaking
a merry counter-clocking chase
big blow blowing into town

white sheets blanket
frozen flower beds

in the treetops
bedlam bellows
like locomotives
the roar becomes
a screaming demon
clawing at the house
rattling the windows

ghostly trees
stand shadowed
in walls of whirling white

driving frozen flakes
in slender columns
pulsing by the window

radiators hiss and snap
televisions show and tell
weather ladies wrapped
in winter burkas
peer from slits
between scarves and hoods
and tout the falling snow
today's blizzard
is brought to you by . . .

at airports
flights are grounded
while in our yard
the flights continue
in the driving white
birds flutter
crowds of wings gather
'round the bulging feeders

in the house
lights are flickering
power throttled by the storm
and so it goes
and so it blows
as big blow
blows through town

Homeless Veterans

for Jim

a spring morning
gray cool and windy
a stadium concrete heavy
stands empty

outside
a festive crowd
is gathering
some bedecked
in starry striped bandanas
others doff
Dr Suess top-hats
of red blue white
while others stride along
in soccer socks
that look like
spinning barber poles

flags on
hand-held poles
furl and unfurl
snapping
in the stadium's
swirling gusts

chattering girls
in cheerleader outfits
flock by
waving balloons and
silver-stranded pompoms

run the stadium stairs
raise money for
wounded warriors
without homes
says a booming voice
bursting
from an unseen speaker
and echoing
round the coliseum

now let's take a moment
to hear
our national anthem

Emma
blonde blue-eyed
and looking chilled
pierces
the cavernous silence

ohhh oh say can you see . . .

the voice booms resonates
belying her fourteen years
coming to the final high notes
applause begins to build
and when she nails
the final note
cheers explode
like crackers in July

runners with cheeks
like reddened apples
bounce in place
anxious to get started
another minute
and they're off

red blue and white
a happy human snake
winds up and down
the stadium stairs
loudspeakers blast out
fifties rock tunes

Little Richard wonders
once again
what's up with Maybelline
why can't she be true . . .

meanwhile the crowd
practices alchemy
changing footsteps
into dollars to build
homes for injured soldiers

that afternoon
I drive to visit Jim
who is sitting in his wheelchair
in a hospital for veterans

returning
home from combat
in Vietnam
horror hardened
rejected

called a baby killer

searing images of war
burned in memory
fodder for the nightmares
that gallop
through his sleep

we spend hours
sorting photos
of faraway loved ones

pausing over each
to visit in his memory
he picks the best
we pin his family
on the wall

I left him
sitting by the window
in warmth and light
sprigs of green
are pushing through
winter's brown and yellow

in the fields outside
voices in the distance
kids are playing soccer

The Primo Protector

for Susan

The Gods of Fairness at Feeders gathered at their Imperium in the clouds to consider the cries of bluebirds, finches, and black-capped chickadees . . . it seems they've been starving, denied their fair share of dry mealworms, hard and soft seeds of safflower, and shelled sunflower seeds. Outraged—the Gods agree to take action—appoint a protector.

After an exhaustive search of all earthly domains, they settled on Susan. Susan is unflagging, an implacable foe of bullying birds, tail-flagging squirrels, or any tormentor bringing grief and starvation to the birdland in our backyard.

I've seen Susan in action, she's—a primo protector—a force on the scale of the incoming tide, relentless, like Don from La Mancha attacking the windmills, or Copperfield's Betsy damning the donkeys off her English green. I've seen Susan on guard at our sliding glass door, ready to charge for an hour, even more.

At the sight of a starling, squirrel, or modo, snatching seeds from the port of a feeder, the heavy glass door opens wide with a bang, and Susan strides forth with clapping and shouting *git, git*, condemning the villains to the tenth circle of Hell, and if that doesn't do it, she'll pick up a stick, or a tennis ball yellow, or whatever's at hand, flinging it well wide . . . and short of its mark.

Blouse of Serious Black

for Anna

the sun
is warming
our home today
those bars of light
coming through
the slats in
the Venetian blinds
never made a sound
when they fell
on the floor
but there they are
lying in alternating
bands of light and dark
like a stairway to . . .

and clothes
shirts socks
and underwear
are hung from racks
. . . without a trial
and drying
in front of the
gas fired place
but they'll
soon rise again
and take their place
as a skin on skin

the wind in the trees
is humming
and Sonos is bringing me
Bach
he's in suite number one
with a cello

a vision is playing
in my world within
. . . our granddaughter
Anna

who plays the cello
and runs half marathons
is preparing for a concert
wearing a musician's
blouse of serious black
hair parted in the middle
drawn tight in a bun
and bound in back
by a ribbon of black

her face a soft smile
her eyes looking down
her lips gently pressed
in purpose
releasing the clasp
of a chain binding
a small heart of gold

The Mother

for Mum

it's the duty
of every man
and every woman
to write the story
of 'the Mother'
so said the poet
Allen Grossman
but 'the Mother'
is not my mother
my mother is Mum

in her middle years
Mum
and her husband Joe
a good man
who worked at
the Boston Navy Yard
lived with me
my six sisters
and the ghost of my
dead brother Tom
on the second floor
of a two family house
at 68 Thetford Ave

old lady Johnson
and her daughter
large Marge
lived on the first floor

sometimes I'd go
to the cellar
to fill the kerosene jug
for our kitchen stove
I was ten
carrying the jug back up
to the second floor
was like lugging
my brother Tom
back from the grave

the stove
was black cast iron
solid and steady
and supplied us
with comfort and warmth
as Mum often did

in the fifth grade
sitting in my classroom
at Robert Swan
elementary school
from time to time
I'd peek at
the large round clock
on the wall
where the big hand
raced past the little hand
until they met at twelve
when the clock
seemed to hold up a finger
to make a point
and say—
it's lunchtime boyo

I thanked God
and the clock
for my liberation
and bolted off to home
just down the street
at 68 Thetford Avenue

Mum
not much taller than I
her hair already white
stood at the black iron stove

she wore a house dress and
an apron around her waist
a grilled cheese sandwich
sizzled in the frying pan
Campbell's tomato soup
was warm in a bowl

at 12:15 the radio spoke
and invited us into the world
of Helen Trent
and her endless romance
with the hapless
but ever faithful Gil Whitney

as always
when entering Helen's world
we are reminded
Helen though mocked by life
her hopes broken and dashed
against the rocks of despair
fought back bravely
successfully
to prove
what so many women
long to prove
that because a woman
is 35 or more

*romance in life
need not be over
that romance . . .*

we never did find out why
in spite of proving her case
so successfully
by stringing along
her long-suffering suiter
Gil Whitney
she never did
consummate the affair
maybe Gil was gelded
or maybe Mum
just put the kibosh
on that episode

no sooner had Helen Trent
moved on
continuing to prove her point
with Gil trailing behind
when Our Gal Sunday
washed in on the air waves

when entering
Our Gal Sunday's world
the question was always
*can this girl Sunday
from a little mining town
in the west
find happiness
as the wife of a wealthy
and titled Englishman*

the very good
very handsome
very rich
titled and also entitled
Englishman was
Lord Henry Brinthrope

he had come to
Sunday's little town in the west
to check on his silver mine
and fell for Sunday
and her formidable beauty

I took another bite
of my grilled cheese
and sucked up the last
of the Campbell's soup

like most kids my age
in working class families
I had a shaky grip
on the concept
of social standing
but this much seemed clear

Sunday
a girl from a little mining town
in the west
was out of her league
in cozying up
to Lord Brinthrope
and thinking of becoming

Lady Brinthrope
but even then I was disposed
to root for the underdog—

I swallowed the rest of my
grilled cheese
planted a filial buss
on my Mum's cheek
and hurried off
to the Robert Swan

that we should all write
of 'the Mother' sounds
like a metaphysical theme
or perhaps other more
remote cosmic concerns
. . . like ideas that probe
the nature and source
of female fecundity
the essence of femininity
or patterns of life
beyond DNA

well my Mum's story
is more earthly
she was born
in New Waterford
a little coal mining town
in Cape Breton's northeast
not far from the Cabot Trail
of New Scotland
—Nova Scotia
where the wind blows west
off the Gulf Stream

she lived with six siblings
three of each gender
an overwhelmed mother
and a father named Tom
whom she loved
it was his name that she gave
to her first born son
a son who soon after died

at six she
was packed off
from New Waterford
to nearby Big Pond
to live with her mother's
sweet sister Katie
easing her mother's burdens
while severing Mum
from her family
but she was happy
at Katie's farm in Big Pond

when Katie was married
Mum now thirteen
was returned to her family
where she was treated
like Cinderella
without the Prince

she was assigned
many duties including
shining her brother's shoes
and having them ready
when the brothers
rose in the morning

she loved the brothers
a bright apple bunch
in her mother's eyes
but she had hopes
and ambitions too
she wished
that she could go
to the university
like all three of
her brothers

she was seventeen
when she set out for Boston
to work
easing the housekeeping
burdens of the blessed
lace curtain Irish

on her days off
she could be seen
in the company
of strong silent Joe
who was a bit unfinished
compared to
Lord Brinthrope
but who would become
Joe
father of eight

a good man who worked
at the Boston Navy Yard
and lived with my Mum
at 68 Thetford Avenue

I Love

for Susan

yes I love you
when I crack and
poach the eggs
make the coffee
and cut the fruit
giving you the best
and freshest cuts

I love you
when I prepare
the ground
for your new garden
and when you ask
but never nag

I love you when
I bury my nose
in the softness
of my still warm
folded laundry
inhaling a freshness
like springtime
and a scent like
a newborn's breath

I love you
when you take me
touring your gardens
and introduce me

to your friends
black eyed susan
lady georgia mauna loa
and all the other
lovely ladies
who flourish
and flower there
in gowns of baby blue
hot pink ruby red
and white

About the Author

Joe Leary was born in Boston, grew up in Franklin, MA, and still lives there. He has written for pleasure all his life. He has published many articles and book chapters in the field of dental implantology, a discipline he practiced as part of his profession. He started writing poetry in 2017. This is his first book of poetry.

His non-literary experience includes service as a Marine, an FBI agent, and a Periodontist, as well as wide variety of less visible, but nevertheless important tasks: floor washer, painter (of walls), mill worker, grocery clerk, chicken farmhand, etc.

With such varied life experience, he comes with a rich source of material for his poetry. Themes of this work are wide-ranging and include: humor, family relationships, self-knowledge, and the beauty of nature.

About the Illustrator

Beginning in childhood, Jack Leary continued a lifetime of creativity. He started in the art world, essentially self-taught, earning a place as the acknowledged class artist in high school. Later he studied at the Boston Museum School, eventually setting out on a solo journey that took him across Europe, the Baltics, and Asia. He spent months in India.

Returning to the United States (he crisscrossed the country, continuing to Mexico), sketching and painting all along the way; he eventually settled in Heber City, Utah, for many years. His work includes painting in multiple mediums: stained glass, wood carvings, collages, and reliefs in wood and paper. Much of it can be seen on his website. He's had shows in Boston, North Carolina, California, and Utah.

Visit his website at:
jackfleary.com